The Rosary in the Steps of the Gospel

Dom Jean Guilmard, O.S.B.
a Monk of the Benedictine Abbaye St. Pierre
Solesmes, France

Translated from the French
by Oblates of Solesmes

The Rosary in the Steps of the Gospel

Featuring the Mysteries of Light

Foreword by
Theodore Cardinal McCarrick, Ph.D., D.D.

Christian Classics
from Ave Maria Press, Inc.   Notre Dame, IN

NIHIL OBSTAT:
Rev. Msgr. Glenn D. Gardner, J.C.D.
Censor Librorum

IMPRIMATUR:
† Most Rev. Charles V. Grahmann
Bishop of Dallas

March 7, 2003

The Nihil Obstat and Imprimatur are official declarations that the
material reviewed is free of doctrinal or moral error. No implication is
contained therein that those granting the Nihil Obstat and Imprimatur
agree with the contents, opinions, or statements expressed.

Acknowledgments

Send all inquiries to:
Christian Classics
P.O. Box 428
Notre Dame, IN 46556
Website: **www.avemariapress.com**

Printed in the United States of America

Library of Congress Control Number: 2003102134

ISBN 0-87061-229-8

Foreword

Pope John Paul II has given many gifts to the Church: his deep theological insights, his courage, his vision. History may tell us that one of his greatest gifts was presented in the apostolic letter on the Rosary of the Virgin Mary when he enunciated the Mysteries of Light, relating this beautiful devotion to the Mother of God even more closely to the Good News of the Gospel proclaimed by her divine Son.

I would venture that no Pope in history has had a greater devotion to the Blessed Virgin Mary than the present Holy Father. His faithful dedication to the Rosary is a gift to the Church, and now he has indeed made that gift more powerful and more able to teach us the mystery of our salvation. The Holy Father saw that the Rosary as we have used it for our meditation over the century has not focused enough on the public life of Jesus and on the light these historic events cast on the role of our Savior.

When he calls these new additions "The Mysteries of Light," he invites us to find more light for our own journey by meditating on the wonderful journey of the life of the Lord. I find great consolation in these mysteries as well as a great challenge to holiness that is made to us all. We do not cease to see Our Lady's presence in all of these special moments, but here we focus on her Divine Son, as she herself would always have us do.

I recommend *The Rosary in the Steps of the Gospel,* featuring the new Mysteries of Light. The clausular method used in this book brings us closer to the life of Christ as it follows directly from the Gospels. In responding to the wisdom and insight of Pope John Paul II, I pray that many of us will be inspired by this unique format of the Rosary as it is composed by a monk of Abbaye St. Pierre, the Benedictine monastery of Solesmes in France. May it bring much grace and confidence to our lives in Christ through these reflections on the Gospel and the prayers of the Blessed Virgin Mary.

Theodore Cardinal McCarrick
Archbishop of Washington, D.C.

Preface

THIS SECOND EDITION of *The Rosary in the Steps of the Gospel* is motivated by the apostolic letter *Rosarium Virginis Mariae,* in which Pope John Paul II has proposed to the Church the addition of five new Mysteries of Light to the centuries-old devotion of the most holy Rosary:

> "The center of gravity in the *Hail Mary,* the hinge as it were which joins its two parts, is *the name of Jesus.* Sometimes, in hurried recitation, this center of gravity can be overlooked, and with it the connection to

the mystery of Christ being contemplated. Yet it is precisely the emphasis given to the name of Jesus and to his mystery that is the sign of a meaningful and fruitful recitation of the Rosary. Pope Paul VI drew attention, in his Apostolic Exhortation *Marialis Cultus,* to the custom in certain regions of highlighting the name of Christ by the addition of a clause referring to the mystery being contemplated. This is a praiseworthy custom, especially during public recitation. It gives forceful expression to our faith in Christ, directed to the different moments of the Redeemer's life. It is at once *a profession of faith* and an aid in concentrating our meditation, since it facilitates the process of assimilation to the mystery of Christ inherent in the repetition of the *Hail Mary.* When we repeat the name of Jesus—the only name given to us by which we may hope for salvation (cf. *Acts* 4:12)—in close association with the name of his Blessed Mother, almost as if it were done at her suggestion, we set out on a path of assimilation meant to help us enter more deeply into the life of Christ."

John Paul II,
Rosarium Virginis Mariae (33)
October 16, 2002

Introduction

THE ROSARY is a special privilege offered to us by the Church. Under the guidance of Our Lady, we can learn to contemplate the mysteries of the Redemptive Incarnation. Who can teach us to meditate better than the Blessed Virgin—she who "treasured all these words and pondered them in her heart"? (Luke 2:19)

Ever since this devotion to Our Lady has been in use, numerous ways of saying the Rosary have been proposed and practiced, each one with its own particular merits and drawbacks. Among them, the method of the "clausulas" deserves attention as it allows for a deeper meditation on each of the great mysteries of our faith. The clausular method of praying the Rosary—like all other methods—recalls each mystery in its broadest sense, which is the very essence of the Rosary, but at the same time it details the main episodes with their various aspects.

At the beginning of the fifteenth century, the clausular method appeared for the first time in Trier under the influence of a Carthusian friar, Dominic of Prussia. Widespread at that time, it has remained in use in German-speaking countries and is now enjoying a revival in France.

Experience has shown that many people prefer using clausulas, which gives them a feeling of conversing with Our Lady. Such is the nature of the clausulas offered in these pages. Their length does not exceed that of the second part of the Ave Maria, and the recitation of the Rosary is no longer than before. Moreover, they follow faithfully the chrono-logical order of each mystery, which helps to memorize them. Finally, we have added certain episodes, which although not included in the Gospels are nevertheless part of church tradition and are cherished by the faithful.

These include Jesus falling three times on His ascent to Calvary, His encounter with His mother and Veronica, and so forth.

With practice, this method can soon be used without the text. The chronological order not only helps one to memorize the clausulas and avoid distractions, it makes this form of prayer more lively, appealing, and fruitful.

Dom Jean Guilmard, O.S.B.

How to Pray the Rosary Using the Clausular Method

𝕭EGIN THE ROSARY with the Apostles' Creed, which is said on the crucifix, and follow this with the *Our Father,* three *Hail Marys,* and a *Gloria* (Glory be to the Father, . . . etc). Begin each decade of the Rosary with the *Our Father.* Follow this with the first half of the *Hail Mary* (Hail Mary, full of grace . . . blessed is the fruit of your womb, Jesus). This is then followed by the ten numbered clausulas. Finish each decade with the traditional second half of the *Hail Mary* (Holy Mary, Mother of God . . . now and at the hour of our death. Amen). This arrangement illustrates the essence of each of the mysteries as you pray the Rosary. Finally, complete each decade with the *Gloria.*

The Sign of the Cross

IN THE NAME of the Father, and of the Son, and of the Holy Spirit, Amen.

The Apostles' Creed

I BELIEVE IN GOD, the Father almighty, Creator of heaven and earth; and in Jesus Christ, His only Son, Our Lord: who was conceived by the Holy Spirit, born of the Virgin Mary, suffered under Pontius Pilate, was crucified, died, and was buried. He descended into hell; the third day He rose again from the dead. He ascended into heaven, and sits at the right hand of God, the Father almighty; from thence He shall come to judge the living and the dead. I believe in the Holy Spirit, the holy Catholic Church, the communion of saints, the forgiveness of sins, the resurrection of the body, and life everlasting. Amen.

The Lord's Prayer

OUR FATHER, who art in heaven, hallowed be thy name; thy kingdom come; thy will be done on earth as it is in heaven. Give us this day our daily bread; and forgive us our trespasses, as we forgive those who trespass against us; and lead us not into temptation, but deliver us from evil. Amen.

The Hail Mary

HAIL MARY, full of grace; the Lord is with you; blessed are you among women, and blessed is the fruit of your womb, Jesus. Holy Mary, Beloved daughter of the Father, pray for us sinners, now and at the hour of our death. Amen.

HAIL MARY, full of grace; the Lord is with you; blessed are you among women, and blessed is the fruit of your womb, Jesus. Holy Mary, Mother of our Savior, pray for us sinners now and at the hour of our death. Amen.

HAIL MARY, full of grace; the Lord is with you; blessed are you among women, and blessed is the fruit of your womb, Jesus. Holy Mary, Spouse of the Holy Spirit, pray for us sinners, now and at the hour of our death. Amen.

The Gloria

GLORY BE to the Father, and to the Son, and to the Holy Spirit; as it was in the beginning, is now, and ever shall be, world without end. Amen.

Days of the Week

The Joyful, Luminous, Sorrowful, and Glorious Mysteries are said on the following days of the week:

Monday	—	Joyful
Tuesday	—	Sorrowful
Wednesday	—	Glorious
Thursday	—	Luminous
Friday	—	Sorrowful
Saturday	—	Joyful
Sunday	—	Glorious

The Joyful Mysteries

Sixteenth-century statue at the entrance to
the Abbatial Church in Solesmes, France.
It is one of the few statues of the Virgin where
she is holding the infant Jesus in her right arm.

The Annunciation

OUR FATHER, . . . from evil. Amen.

HAIL MARY, *full of grace, the Lord is with you, blessed are you among women and blessed is the fruit of your womb, Jesus.*

1. The Angel Gabriel, as the messenger of God, greeted you in such a wondrous fashion at your home at Nazareth.

2. You were so troubled in your humility and pondered the significance of this greeting.

3. The Angel reassured and enlightened you, announcing that God had chosen you to be the mother of the Messiah.

4. You were reminded by the Angel of God's wondrous promise that the Messiah would be born of the House of David.

5. You questioned with prudence, "How can this be, since I am a virgin?" (Luke 1:34) meaning thereby that you vowed to remain so.

6. The Angel replied: "The Holy Spirit will come upon you, and the power of the Most High will overshadow you." (Luke 1:35)

7. The Angel revealed the wonder of wonders, that the child to be born to you would be the true son of God.

8. The Angel gave you as proof of this message, the coming miraculous motherhood of your cousin, Elizabeth.

9. Fully accepting God's plan you answered: "Here am I, the servant of the Lord, Let it be with me according to your word." (Luke 1:38)

10. Jesus, at that very instant, in an act of perfect obedience to His Father, became flesh in your virginal womb.

HOLY MARY, *Mother of God, obtain for us the grace of a joyous and loving submission to God's will, and pray for us sinners, now and at the hour of our death. Amen.*

GLORY BE to the Father, . . . Amen.

The Visitation

OUR FATHER, . . . from evil. Amen.

HAIL MARY, *full of grace, the Lord is with you, blessed are you among women and blessed is the fruit of your womb, Jesus.*

1. Jesus within you inspired you to visit without delay your cousin Elizabeth, to share her joy and assist her.

2. Jesus was light within you as you climbed the hills of Judea.

3. The hidden presence of Jesus made John the Baptist move with joy in his mother's womb.

4. The Holy Spirit revealed to Elizabeth the real meaning of this sign so that she greeted you as the Mother of her Lord.

5. Elizabeth hailed you with these loving praises: "Blessed are you among women, and blessed is the fruit of your womb." (Luke 1:42)

6. Jesus inspired you to say with joy: "My soul magnifies the Lord, and my spirit rejoices in God my Savior." (Luke 1:46–47)

7. Jesus, by His hidden presence, sanctified the last months of Elizabeth's waiting for the birth of John the Baptist.

8. Zachariah hailed in his newborn son, the precursor of Jesus, true Light of the World and the Sun of Justice.

9. You brought Jesus back to Nazareth, a hidden treasure now heavier to bear, meditating all the while on these wondrous events.

10. Joseph was chosen to serve as earthly Father to Jesus by his humble obedience to the Angel who said: "Joseph, son of David, do not be afraid to take Mary as your wife." (Matthew 1:20)

HOLY MARY, *Mother of God, obtain for us the grace of a fervent charity for others, and pray for us sinners, now and at the hour of our death. Amen.*

GLORY BE to the Father, . . . Amen.

The Nativity

OUR FATHER, . . . from evil. Amen.

HAIL MARY, *full of grace, the Lord is with you, blessed are you among women and blessed is the fruit of your womb, Jesus.*

    1. You carried Jesus for six more months with love, so happy to feel Him grow within you.

    2. Jesus was to be born in Bethlehem where you were led by Providence through an edict of Caesar Augustus.

    3. You and Joseph were obliged to bring Jesus, Creator of the Universe, into the world in a lowly stable.

    4. You received Jesus with more love and tenderness, joy, admiration, and thanksgiving than any other mother has ever borne for her child.

    5. You nursed and mothered Jesus, wrapped Him in swaddling clothes, and laid Him in a manger, while adoring in Him the Son of God.

    6. You offered Jesus to Joseph's adoration, as well as to his fatherly tenderness.

7. The birth of Jesus was acclaimed by a choir of Angels: "Glory to God in the highest heaven, and on earth peace among those whom he favors." (Luke 2:14)

8. You presented Jesus to the shepherds to adore, receiving from them humble gifts.

9. The Magi, guided by the star, came to adore Jesus as the great King, both Eternal God and mortal man, with the symbolic gifts of gold, frankincense, and myrrh.

10. Wonders were told of Jesus, which you cherished in the constant meditation of your heart.

HOLY MARY, *Mother of God, obtain for us the grace of a true and sincere detachment from the goods of this world, and pray for us sinners, now and at the hour of our death. Amen.*

GLORY BE to the Father, . . . Amen.

The Presentation

OUR FATHER, . . . from evil. Amen.

HAIL MARY, *full of grace, the Lord is with you, blessed are you among women and blessed is the fruit of your womb, Jesus.*

1. You saw with an aching heart the redeeming blood of Jesus flow for the first time eight days after His birth.

2. You gave to Jesus, according to the divine command received through the Angel, the holy name that means Yahveh Savior.

3. Thirty-three days later, as a young mother, radiant with happiness and pride, you brought Jesus to the temple in Jerusalem.

4. In the joy and sincerity of your heart, you offered Jesus to His Father with the premonition that He would one day be the sacrificial lamb.

5. You followed Jesus along the path of humility and obedience in submitting yourself to the rite of purification.

6. You placed Jesus in the arms of Simeon, a man of great age, who, inspired by the Holy Spirit, had come to the temple.

7. Simeon received Jesus with happiness, exclaiming: "Master, now you are dismissing your servant in peace, according to your word." (Luke 2:29)

8. Simeon acclaimed Jesus as the Light of Nations and the Glory of his people Israel.

9. Simeon foretold that one day, because of Jesus, a sword would pierce your heart.

10. Prophet Anna also said wonderful things of Him, which you cherished in your heart.

HOLY MARY, *Mother of God, obtain for us the grace of a perfect purity of body, mind, and heart; and pray for us sinners, now and at the hour of our death. Amen.*

GLORY BE to the Father, . . . Amen.

The Hidden Life of Jesus

OUR FATHER, . . . from evil. Amen.

HAIL MARY, *full of grace, the Lord is with you, blessed are you among women and blessed is the fruit of your womb, Jesus.*

   1. You were obliged to flee into Egypt to save Jesus from Herod's cruel jealousy.

   2. You watched over Jesus, a happy child learning to speak and walk in that land of exile.

   3. When told by the Angel, you brought Jesus back to Nazareth where He continued to grow in age and grace.

   4. You took Jesus, when He was twelve, on His first pilgrimage to Jerusalem, where He was radiant with joy, and you shared his happiness.

   5. You and Joseph sought Jesus for three days, overcome with anguish and sorrow.

   6. You were so happy to recover Jesus amidst the Doctors of the Law, who marveled at the wisdom of His replies.

7. Jesus answered your questions tinged with reproach: "Did you not know that I must be in my Father's house?" (Luke 2:49)

8. Jesus, whose response you and Joseph did not understand at the time, but which became clear at his Passion.

9. Jesus, who returned with you to Nazareth where he remained humbly obedient, sharing an ever-deeper intimacy of soul.

10. Jesus, whom you helped to grow in knowledge and wisdom, faithfully passing on to him the heritage of the children of Israel.

𝕳OLY MARY, *Mother of God, obtain for us the love of a humble and hidden life, totally dedicated to the will of God. Amen.*

GLORY BE to the Father, . . . Amen.

The Luminous Mysteries

Statue of Saint John the Baptist sculpted by
Dom Jacques Froger, a monk of Solesmes,
on the occasion of the Jubilee of Abbot
Dom Cozien in 1946.

Baptism of Christ

OUR FATHER, . . . from evil. Amen.

HAIL MARY, *full of grace, the Lord is with you, blessed are you among women and blessed is the fruit of your womb, Jesus.*

1. Jesus replied to John, "Let it be so now; for it is proper for us in this way to fulfill all rightousness." (Matthew 3:14)

2. Jesus, the innocent one, in descending into the Jordan, is made "sin for us."

3. Jesus, who on coming out of the river, saw the heavens open and the Spirit descend upon Him.

4. Jesus, of whom the Father has said, "This is my Son, the Beloved, with whom I am very well pleased." (Matthew 3:17)

5. Jesus of whom John proclaimed, "I myself have seen and have testified that this is the Son of God." (John 1:34)

6. Jesus, of whom John gave witness, "I saw the Spirit descending from heaven like a dove and it remained on him." (John 1:32)

7. Jesus, whom John named, "the Lamb of God who takes away the sin of the world."(John 1:29)

8. Jesus met His first disciples on the banks of the Jordan.

9. Jesus left the banks of the Jordan filled with the Holy Spirit.

10. Jesus, who was then led by the Father and the Holy Spirit to begin His ministry.

HOLY MARY, Mother of God, help us to be faithful to the baptism which we have also received as beloved children of the Father, and pray for us sinners, now and at the hour of our death. Amen.

GLORY BE to the Father, . . . Amen.

The Wedding Feast of Cana

OUR FATHER, . . . from evil. Amen.

HAIL MARY, *full of grace, the Lord is with you, blessed are you among women and blessed is the fruit of your womb, Jesus.*

    1. Jesus wished to sanctify marriage by His presence at the wedding.

    2. Jesus accomplished His first sign that He was the Messiah.

    3. Jesus, who at Cana revealed Himself as the bridegroom who gives to the Church her spouse.

    4. Jesus to whom Mary guides us, "Do whatever he tells you." (John 2:5)

    5 Jesus, who at Cana as at Calvary, addressed His mother as "woman."

    6. Jesus rewarded the faith of His mother with the work of His first miracle.

    7. Jesus, who at Cana made allusion for the first time to "the Hour" of His Passion.

    8. Jesus, through the wine offered at Cana, signified the gift of the Holy Spirit upon the children of the Kingdom.

9. Jesus, in changing the water into wine, prefigured the mystery of the Eucharist.

10. Jesus, who at the wedding of Cana, "revealed His glory; and his disciples believed in him." (John 2:11)

HOLY MARY, Mother of God, may your presence in the center of Christian families cause them to imitate, by their chaste and fruitful love, the union of Christ and the Church, and pray for us sinners, now and at the hour of our death. Amen.

GLORY BE to the Father, . . . Amen.

Proclamation of the Kingdom and Call to Conversion

Ⓞ UR FATHER, . . . from evil. Amen.

HAIL MARY, *full of grace, the Lord is with you, blessed are you among women and blessed is the fruit of your womb, Jesus.*

1. Jesus, before announcing the Kingdom of God, withdrew to the desert to pray.

2. Jesus, who in Galilee announced the Kingdom and proclaimed the urgent need to repent.

3. Jesus ascended the mountain for His inaugural discourse—the Beatitudes of the Kingdom of God.

4. Jesus, who as a sign of the coming of the Kingdom, healed the sick and expelled evil spirits.

5. Jesus revealed to the children the secrets of the Kingdom in parables.

6. Jesus, who traversing Palestine, revealed the infinite mercy of the Father for sinners.

7. Jesus taught His disciples the essential prayer, the Our Father.

8. Jesus forgives the sins of all who approach Him with a humble faith.

9. Jesus, the light of the world, revealed Himself as "the way, and the truth, and the life." (John 14:6)

10. Jesus, who tells us, "Go into all the world and proclaim the good news to the whole creation." (Mark 16:15)

HOLY MARY, Mother of God, open our hearts to all the words which your son has sown on human soil, that they may become the harvest of the Kingdom, and pray for us sinners, now and at the hour of our death. Amen.

GLORY BE to the Father, . . . Amen.

The Transfiguration

Ⓞ UR FATHER, . . . from evil. Amen.

HAIL MARY, *full of grace, the Lord is with you, blessed are you among women and blessed is the fruit of your womb, Jesus.*

1. Jesus on Mount Tabor wished to strengthen His disciples before the scandal of the Passion.

2. Jesus, ascending the mountain, prayed on Mount Tabor and was transfigured there.

3. Jesus chose Peter, James, and John as witnesses of His transfiguration.

4. Jesus briefly let shine forth the splendor of His divinity.

5. Jesus on Mount Tabor spoke with Moses and Elijah, witnesses to the prophecies of the Old Testament.

6. Jesus, to whom a voice came from the cloud of glory revealing, "This is my Son, my Chosen; listen to him!" (Luke 9:35)

7. Jesus, to whom Peter in ecstasy suggested, "Let us make three dwellings, one

for you, one for Moses, and one for Elijah."
(Luke 9:33)

8. Jesus, who in his transfiguration revealed to us the glory of our future resurrection.

9. Jesus, as they were coming down from Mount Tabor, firmly enjoined His disciples to keep the transfiguration secret until His resurrection.

10. Jesus, descending the mountain, announced to His disciples three times His coming Passion.

H‌OLY MARY, Mother of God, overshadowed by the power of the Holy Spirit, obtain for us the grace to hear forever the Word of God in the teaching of the Prophets and the Apostles of Jesus, and pray for us sinners, now and at the hour of our death. Amen.

GLORY BE to the Father, . . . Amen.

Institution of the Eucharist

OUR FATHER, . . . from evil. Amen.

HAIL MARY, *full of grace, the Lord is with you, blessed are you among women and blessed is the fruit of your womb, Jesus.*

1. Jesus in the multiplication of the loaves prefigured innumerable Eucharists throughout the world.

2. Jesus, who by His Passover completed and perfected the sacrifices of the Old Testament.

3. Jesus washed the feet of His apostles as a sign of humility and fraternal love.

4. Jesus, who in saying, "This is my body . . . . this is my blood," (Matthew 26:26, 27) instituted thereby the sacrament of His real presence, which never ceases to remain with us.

5. Jesus shed His blood for the multitude in the remission of sin.

6. Jesus, who to establish the Eucharist instituted a new priesthood in saying, "Do this in remembrance of me." (Luke 22:19)

7. Jesus, after supper offered up to His Father the most perfect thanksgiving, His sacerdotal prayer.

8. Jesus unites with His mother in the Eucharist through the priestly ministry of the beloved disciple.

9. Jesus is always present in the Eucharist for our adoration.

10. Jesus, who in this sacrament gives to us the memorial of His Passion, fills us with grace, and gives us the promise of our resurrection.

HOLY MARY, Mother of God, help us to participate with more fervor and love in the mystery of the Holy Eucharist, and pray for us sinners, now and at the hour of our death. Amen.

GLORY BE to the Father, . . . Amen.

The Sorrowful Mysteries

Fifteenth-century statue of the Pietá, from the
Abbatial Church in Solesmes, France.

The Agony

Ⓞ̶UR FATHER, . . . from evil. Amen.

HAIL MARY, *full of grace, the Lord is with you, blessed are you among women and blessed is the fruit of your womb, Jesus.*

1. Jesus began to tremble with fear and anguish on the way to Gethsemani.

2. Jesus chose three of His most beloved Apostles, Peter, James, and John, to be the only witnesses to His agony.

3. Jesus, at the beginning of His agony, prayed: "My Father, if it is possible, let this cup pass from me." (Matthew 26:39)

4. Jesus, coming back to His Apostles for solace, was saddened to find them asleep.

5. Jesus, whose supplication became more pressing, again prayed: "Abba, Father, for you all things are possible; remove this cup from me." (Mark 14:36)

6. Jesus was so overwhelmed with anguish and torment that His sweat became as drops of blood.

7. Jesus was comforted by an Angel sent from His Father when He was at the limit of His human strength.

8. Jesus, in a third prayer, fully consented with all His heart to save us by His passion, saying: "Father, ... not my will but yours be done." (Luke 22:42)

9. Jesus, giving Judas a last chance of salvation, accepted from him the kiss of betrayal.

10. Jesus, having given a last proof of His power, let Himself be seized and saw all His disciples abandon Him.

ℌOLY MARY, *Mother of God, obtain for us the grace of a profound and sincere repentance for our sins, and pray for us sinners, now and at the hour of our death. Amen.*

GLORY BE to the Father, . . . Amen.

The Trial

OUR FATHER, . . . from evil. Amen.

HAIL MARY, *full of grace, the Lord is with you, blessed are you among women and blessed is the fruit of your womb, Jesus.*

1. Jesus was brought to the house of Annas, the father-in-law of the high priest, for an enquiry to prove the truth of the accusation against Him.

2. Jesus had profound sorrow to see Peter, who had been chosen as leader of the apostles, deny three times that he was His disciple.

3. Jesus replied with meekness to the servant who struck Him on the face, "If I have spoken wrongly, testify to the wrong. But if I have spoken rightly, why do you strike me?" (John 18:23)

4. Jesus was brought before the high priest Caiaphas and the scribes and elders, and when asked if He was the Messiah, affirmed "You have said so." (Matthew 26:64)

5. Jesus, because of His affirmation, was condemned to death for blasphemy, insulted, mocked, and beaten.

6. Jesus was then led to Pilate, the Roman governor, who asked Him if He was a king: "My kingdom is not from this world. . . . You say that I am a king." (John 18:36, 37)

7. Jesus was found innocent by Pilate who was too cowardly to acquit Him and sent Him on to King Herod.

7. Jesus, whom the soldiers crowned with thorns in a cruel and sacrilegious parody, yet prophetic, of a royal coronation.

8. Jesus was presented to the crowd by Pilate as "the king of the Jews," to which they cried out: "Crucify him!" (Mark 15:12, 13)

9. Jesus, who the crowds ultimately condemned by demanding Pilate release not him, but rather the notorious murderer, Barabbas.

10. Jesus, although innocent, was condemned to death on the cross by Pilate in a supreme act of cowardice for fear of losing the Emperor's favor.

HOLY MARY, *Mother of God, obtain for us the grace to follow the ways of justice and truth whatever the judgments of men, and pray for us sinners, now and at the hour of our death. Amen.*

GLORY BE to the Father, . . . Amen.

The Scourging and Crowning with Thorns

OUR FATHER, . . . from evil. Amen.

HAIL MARY, *full of grace, the Lord is with you, blessed are you among women and blessed is the fruit of your womb, Jesus.*

1. Jesus, whom the soldiers took into the Praetorium and gathered around Him the entire cohort.

2. Jesus, whom the soldiers stripped and arrayed in a purple cloak.

3. Jesus, who by the order of Pilate, was cruelly scourged.

4. Jesus, whose physical strength was so weakened, the Romans ignored the Jewish law of forty lashes.

5. Jesus, to whom the soldiers placed a reed in His right hand, a symbol of a royal scepter.

6. Jesus, whom the soldiers mocked, bending their knee before Him, exclaiming, "Hail, King of the Jews!" (Matthew 27:29)

7. Jesus, whose holy face was soiled by the soldiers who spat upon Him.

8. Jesus was struck by the soldiers on the head with a reed.

9. Jesus, whom had been beaten and humiliated, mockingly was honored with a crown of thorns.

10. Jesus, whom Pilate presented to the mob of Jews and said, "Here is your king!" (John 19:14)

𝕳OLY MARY, *Mother of God, obtain for us the grace to understand the necessity of mortification and to accept with submission the humiliations of life, and pray for us sinners, now and at the hour of our death. Amen.*

GLORY BE to the Father, . . . Amen.

The Way of the Cross

OUR FATHER, . . . from evil. Amen.

HAIL MARY, *full of grace, the Lord is with you, blessed are you among women and blessed is the fruit of your womb, Jesus.*

1. Jesus was burdened with the crushing weight of the cross, an instrument of torture so infamous that it was used only for slaves.

2. Jesus fell for the first time but rose—in spite of heavy blows and insults—to accomplish the work of our salvation.

3. Jesus was heartbroken to see His mother in tears on His way to Calvary.

4. Jesus suffered and was humiliated, and the very sight caused your mother's heart cruel grief.

5. Jesus was so deprived of human strength that the soldiers had to command Simon of Cyrene to help carry His cross.

6. Jesus rewarded the holy woman who made a compassionate gesture of pity toward Him.

7. Jesus fell a second time but rose once more—in His infinite love for us—to resume His climb toward Calvary.

8. Jesus, in the midst of such suffering, had the courage to console the women of Jerusalem, and urged them to repentance.

9. Jesus collapsed a third time at the summit of Calvary, so totally exhausted that He was incapable of raising Himself again.

10. Jesus, so brutally stripped of His garments, appeared thus as a victim ready to be sacrificed.

HOLY MARY, *Mother of God, obtain for us the grace to accept with generosity and patience all our anxieties and sufferings, and pray for us sinners, now and at the hour of our death. Amen.*

GLORY BE to the Father, . . . Amen.

Death on the Cross

OUR FATHER, . . . from evil. Amen.

HAIL MARY, *full of grace, the Lord is with you, blessed are you among women and blessed is the fruit of your womb, Jesus.*

1. Jesus endured such unspeakable suffering as His hands were nailed to the crossbeam.

2. Jesus, whose feet had been transfixed on the cross, was then raised up.

3. Jesus, in the midst of such cruel suffering, prayed for His executioners: "Father, forgive them; for they do not know what they are doing." (Luke 23:34)

4. Jesus bequeathed John and all humanity to your motherly tenderness, when He said: "Woman, here is your son." (John 19:26)

5. Jesus spoke to each one of us when He said to John: "Here is your Mother." (John 19:27)

6. Jesus answered the humble plea of the good thief, saying: "Today you will be with me in Paradise." (Luke 23:43)

7. Jesus, at the height of His agony, cried out to His Father in a loud voice: "My God, my God, why have you forsaken me?" (Matthew 27:46)

8. Consummating His sacrifice in a supreme act of love, Jesus cried out: "Father, into your hands I commend my spirit." (Luke 23:46)

9. Jesus, His heart pierced by the lance, was taken down from the cross, and His body was placed into your arms.

10. John, Nicodemus, Joseph of Arimathea, Mary Magdala, and the other holy women helped you lay Jesus in the tomb.

HOLY MARY, *Mother of God, obtain for us the conversion of sinners and the salvation of all your children, and pray for us sinners, now and at the hour of our death. Amen.*

GLORY BE to the Father, . . . Amen.

NI D virtutes q̄ ex vtero matris
mee creuistis mecū, draconis
capita conterentes, coronis
glorie inuicem gratulemur

The Glorious Mysteries

Sixteenth-century depiction of The Coronation of Our Lady, Mary glorified as described in the Apocalypse, the second Eve, from the Abbatial Church at Solesmes, France.

The Resurrection

OUR FATHER, . . . from evil. Amen.

HAIL MARY, *full of grace, the Lord is with you, blessed are you among women and blessed is the fruit of your womb, Jesus.*

1. Jesus arose from the tomb alive and glorious on the morning of the third day as He foretold.

2. Jesus rewarded Mary of Magdala's love by appearing first to her, and choosing her to bring to the Apostles the joyful news of the resurrection.

3. Jesus appeared to the holy women who, with Mary of Magdala, had courageously followed Him to Calvary, and even unto the tomb.

4. Jesus appeared to disciples at Emmaus to reveal to them from Holy Scripture the necessity of redemptive suffering.

5. His disciples, returning in haste to Jerusalem, found the Apostles filled with joy, and said to them: "The Lord has risen indeed, and he has appeared to Simon." (Luke 24:34)

6. Jesus appeared to the ten Apostles at the Cenacle on the evening of Easter, to make them the witnesses of His resurrection, and confer upon them the power to forgive sins.

7. Jesus appeared eight days later to eleven Apostles, and showed His wounds to Thomas, who exclaimed: "My Lord and my God!" (John 20:28)

8. After the second miraculous catch of fish, Jesus appeared mysteriously to seven Apostles and asked Peter three times: "Simon, son of John, do you love me?" (John 21:15ff)

9. Jesus, in response to Peter's profession of love, made him the head of His Church, saying: "Feed my lambs . . . feed my sheep." (John 21:15ff)

10. Jesus appeared to more than five hundred of His disciples to convince us of the historical reality of His Resurrection.

HOLY MARY, *Mother of God, strengthen us in the mystery of the Resurrection, foundation of our entire faith, and pray for us sinners, now and at the hour of our death. Amen.*

GLORY BE to the Father, . . . Amen.

The Ascension

OUR FATHER, . . . from evil. Amen.

HAIL MARY, *full of grace, the Lord is with you, blessed are you among women and blessed is the fruit of your womb, Jesus.*

1. Jesus wished to show Himself for the last time to His disciples gathered together before vanishing from their sight.

2. Jesus began by reproaching them for their slowness in believing the testimony of those who had seen Him risen from the dead.

3. Jesus refused to answer their questions concerning His second coming.

4. Jesus took a last meal with them to give yet another proof of the physical reality of His Resurrection.

5. Jesus entrusted them with their mission saying: "Go, therefore, and make disciples of all nations, baptizing them in the name of the Father and of the Son and of the Holy Spirit." (Matthew 28:19)

6. Jesus promised to confirm the truth of their testimony by miracles and wonders.

7. Jesus filled them with courage and confidence, saying: "I am with you always, to the end of the age." (Matthew 28:20)

8. Jesus blessed them for the last time before ascending to heaven.

9. Jesus sent two Angels to announce to the eleven Apostles that He would return glorious on the last day, as sovereign judge of the living and the dead.

10. The Apostles, returning to Jerusalem, were filled with joy in spite of the pain of separation, because of the great glory into which He had just entered.

HOLY MARY, *Mother of God, strengthen our hope in the treasures that Christ has in store for us, and pray for us sinners, now and at the hour of our death. Amen.*

GLORY BE to the Father, . . . Amen.

Pentecost

OUR FATHER, . . . from evil. Amen.

HAIL MARY, *full of grace, the Lord is with you, blessed are you among women and blessed is the fruit of your womb, Jesus.*

    1. Jesus had often spoken of the Holy Spirit who would come after Him to comfort them and complete His work of salvation.

    2. During the Last Supper, Jesus designated this Paraclete as the Spirit of Truth, the Holy Spirit proceeding from the Father and the Son.

    3. Before ascending into heaven, Jesus told you and the Apostles to await in prayer for the coming of the Holy Spirit.

    4. The Apostles were alerted of this coming by a sound from heaven as of a violent wind, which filled the Cenacle and attracted a large crowd.

    5. The Apostles saw the Holy Spirit descend on each one of them in the shape of tongues of fire, as a sign of the ardent love with which they were to announce the good news.

6. The Apostles began at once to preach to the multitude with zeal, as if they were inebriated with new wine.

7. The Apostles saw the amazement of their listeners when they spoke to each one of them in his own language, a sign that the Gospel should be preached to all nations.

8. Many were pierced to the heart, realizing what they had done by putting Jesus to death, and asked the Apostles what they were to do to be forgiven.

9. Peter answered: "Repent, and be baptized every one of you in the name of Jesus Christ." (Acts 2:38)

10. On that first Pentecost, three thousand souls were bound by faith to Jesus.

HOLY MARY, *Mother of God, obtain for us the grace of an ever-increasing charity, and a greater outpouring of the gifts of the Holy Spirit in our souls, and pray for us sinners, now and at the hour of our death. Amen.*

GLORY BE to the Father, . . . Amen.

The Assumption

OUR FATHER, . . . from evil. Amen.

HAIL MARY, *full of grace, the Lord is with you, blessed are you among women and blessed is the fruit of your womb, Jesus.*

1. You kept His presence in your heart while remaining under the filial protection of John.

2. You continued a more profound intimacy with Jesus over the long years of waiting.

3. You had longed for Jesus' coming with an ever-growing fervor.

4. When the time came, you entrusted your spirit into Jesus' hands in the most perfect act of love.

5. At that very moment, in a vision surpassed only by His own, Jesus revealed to you the infinite splendor of His divine glory.

6. In the same vision, Jesus revealed to you the incomparable splendor of your own holiness.

7. At that very moment, Jesus rendered to you your own body, so that you might share more fully in the mysteries of His Resurrection and Ascension.

8. Jesus placed you for all eternity in the immediate radiance of His divinely glorified humanity.

9. Jesus bestowed upon you this maternal authority even unto heaven, which makes you "the all-powerful Advocate."

10. The Mystical Body of Jesus continues to be the constant object of your vigilance and maternal care.

HOLY MARY, *Mother of God, obtain for us the grace to be ready for Our Lord's call, fully confident in His infinite mercy, and pray for us sinners, now and at the hour of our death. Amen.*

GLORY BE to the Father, . . . Amen.

The Crowning of Our Lady in Heaven

OUR FATHER, . . . from evil. Amen.

HAIL MARY, *full of grace, the Lord is with you, blessed are you among women and blessed is the fruit of your womb, Jesus.*

1. Jesus crowned you Queen of Angels, with your dignity as Mother of God, and placed you infinitely above all the celestial hierarchy.

2. You, Queen of Patriarchs, as the Mother of the Redeemer, are also Mother of all the redeemed.

3. You, Queen of Prophets, brought into the world the Word of God in all its fullness, the Word Incarnate.

4. You, Queen of Apostles, gave the world the Good News in Person, the source of all Truth and Holiness.

5. You, Queen of Martyrs, through the perfect compassion of your maternal heart for the divine sufferings of your son, have more fully glorified God than all those who endured for Him the worst of human sufferings.

6. Queen of Holy Pontiffs, your maternal authority continues to be acknowledged by Him who is the glorious head of the Mystical Body.

7. Queen of Holy Priests, Monks, and Religious, you are more perfectly consecrated than any of those in the service of God and His Divine Son.

8. Queen of Holy Virgins, your purity of body and soul infinitely surpasses theirs in splendor and perfection.

9. Queen of Holy Couples, your chaste union with Joseph is a model of perfect married love, fully spiritualized.

10. Queen of all Saints in Heaven, your glorious crown shines forth with the splendor of all holiness.

HOLY MARY, *Mother of God, become forevermore the Queen of our minds and hearts, and pray for us sinners, now and at the hour of our death. Amen.*

GLORY BE to the Father, . . . Amen.

The Memorare

At the end of the recitation of the rosary

REMEMBER, O most gracious Virgin Mary, that never was it known that anyone who fled to your protection, implored your help, or sought your intercession, was left unaided. Inspired by this confidence, I fly unto you, O Virgin of virgins, my Mother. To you I come, before you I stand, sinful and sorrowful. O Mother of the Word Incarnate, despise not my petitions, but in your mercy, hear and answer me. Amen.

St. Bernard de Clairvaux
1090–1153

There is one kind of prayer . . . that I would like to recall and emphasize to you here: the prayer of contemplation of the mysteries of the Rosary, that "ladder leading us toward Heaven" formed of both mental and vocal prayer, "the two ways that Mary's Rosary offers to Christian souls." It is a form of prayer that the Pope himself practices with zeal and with which he invites you to become united yourselves.

John Paul II,
Homily of April 29, 1979

As a gospel prayer, centered on the mystery of the redemptive Incarnation, the Rosary is therefore a prayer with a clear Christological orientation. . . . The succession of Hail Mary's constitutes the warp on which is woven the contemplation of the mysteries . . . of the Lord's life as seen through the eyes of her who was closest to the Lord.

Paul VI,
Marialis Cultus 46–47
February 2, 1974